HELL ON EARTH! FOR SOME OF US

BY

RUTHIE SPATES

TABLE OF CONTENTS

INTRODUCTION

Are we in the end times as described in the book? of Revelation? Yes and no.

Notice also the time frame references throughout the Book of Revelation, where it talks about things that are 'near at hand'' the ultimate question is that the things that Jesus was talking about in the Olivet Discourse and the Book of Revelation, principally pointing to events that were going to take place in the first century, culminating the destruction of Jerusalem the exile of the Jews. I am not making any predictions about when the world will end. Just know that time is near Mark 13:14

At the end of the sets of seven visions in the book of Revelation- the seven seals, seven trumpets, and seven bowls- John sees a further vision in which a figure identified as Babylon's is destroyed.

Let Us Look At The Stages Of The Apocalypse.

The four Horsemen of the Apocalypse is a metaphor depicting the end of times in the New Testament they describe conquest, war, hunger, and death. Because of the worldliness of Babylon, and because it was a place where the crude they were captive the Kurds often used the name Babylon in the scriptures to repent sin, worldliness, the influence of the devil of the earth, and the spiritual captivity.

Revelation 17:1 that great whore is described, with whom the kings of earth committed fornication she is drunken with the blood of Saints. The mystery of the woman, and the beast that carried her, expounded their destruction.

Reminds me of what Americans had in bed with other countries' repeatedly they have sold their secrets and invited the entire world to come live in American the greatest country in the world the most powerful we have food, and drinks come drink with us, and we will

1

give you access to our world we are drunken with the wine of sin.

America committed a great sin and if she does not repent as a nation, and turn from her wicked ways, we will be doomed!

He will destroy her, the harlot. We are talking about a city Rome, by which the Empire before was civil became Ecclesiastical, is not obscurely signified by this word of which two the exercised cruelly upon bodies of the saints the other upon their souls. The first by human order and policy, the other under the color of the law of God and Religion, raged and imbrued itself with the blood of the godly.

In my life, there have been a lot of unnecessary things that I feel were unjust, and that I have paid a price to write this book.

This book is written in hopes of bringing attention to those who are suffering and being tormented daily.

Those are the ones that live in hell on earth, being judged and sentenced without a trial.

There are somethings that should have killed us, but we still lived until death do us part by God and only God.

The pledge 2019 Covid hell for some of us

When covid hit our world, it was a storm, it was unexpected. We were not prepared to fight, we lost 4.5 million people (about twice the population of New Mexico) worldwide. Experts estimate that each person who dies is significantly grieved by nine others.

It has affected our world, the social impact of grief includes withdrawal, isolation; and conflict due to people having different grieving styles.

Fear gripped the nation, and all over the world storms blew in our lives taking our loved ones there was nothing we could do to stay safe it would take who it pleased.

People were locked into their homes 24/7 some had no one to check on them are get them medical help as caregiver/aid I had a job, to do I could not get sick I washed my hands a lot and I did not have friends to hang out with, so I stay at home.

I took care of the hearts of my older clients they knew I would come and make sure they were ok.

The fear in our hearts was overwhelming, the news played daily of the Numbers going up so fast in New York they had bodies storage in other places on ice, it was hell on earth for those suffering from sickness, both my daughters and three grandsons, granddaughter, got covid.

My husband suffered the most. He was hospitalized and almost lost his life. He said the place was like a spaceship and the body was all over the place. He describes it as hell.

In another world, he had never been to before. He said it was like hell he could hear people talking and codes going off, it was the worst thing I have ever gone through in my life he told me that it still influences his breathing. It was hell in there, he explained.

My husband lived to tell us about his experience with Covid and near death. When we die, we do not get that opportunity to come back and tell if there is a hell or not. I know there is one right here on earth. 2020 was a rough year. We lost lives un-number millions of lives, we lost loved ones, we still remember most on holidays, and birthdays, Christmas, New Year's, every day they spent with them. some of us will move forward, but most of us will never seek help and will live in a state of hell on earth, feeling the pain and suffering the same grift they first felt when told they were gone. They never had a chance to say goodbye.

There was no visit to the hospital and Nursing homes. This

world was not prepared for this unexpected storm. We do not know where their souls are we pray they are with Jesus.

CURSES

I fought many battles, in this life trying to outrun my curses, domestic violence, poverty, and abandoned, rejection with only the love of a mother, and God, whom I would soon meet at the end.

I have finished my course, and I have won. I am at peace, and I know why I had to be in hell to not die in hell.

What beautiful peace when you know the curses are broken within your family you know Jesus saved you!

But if you are marriage to another person that still has the curse on their family it will somehow affect you. We must overall pray for everyone who is under the curse.

We must put an end, to the devil's power, over our minds, God has given, us free, will and choice. We must choose to stay on the course. leaning not to our understanding.

The devil. has killed and taken the souls of our children. We must trust God to save our children, for they only know what they see, in the older generation.

Our world could end any day and as the old saying goes, in hell, you will lift your eyes.

Gambling addictions imprisonment, sex addict, mental illness, poverty, domestic violence, drug addict, child abuse the list goes on and these kinds of behavior can lead to a life of living in hell on earth The curse from generations.

Under the Curse is the power of believing you can, and you shall break the curse.

In Mississippi, we lived in an. old house miles from anyone with dirt roads, trees, the mud so deep you could get stuck just walking, in it after the rain.

We ate, rabbits, chickens, frogs, hogs, and craw fishes, we killed birds, we picked blackberry redberries, and pecans all for free, we lived off the land we had no money my mom worked the land chopping, and picking, cotton. From sun, up to sundown.

1951, we lived on a plantation my mom, and my stepfather worked for the white Bose man.

My mother grew her own food like beans, greens, and sweet potatoes.

We received cheese, flour, packaged meal, flour, lord, to cook I with can. Meat in a can, can peanut butter all free, from us.

From our corrupted government once a month. The poor people called it the government issues, commodity.

We live in a time where black women were submitted to rape, and abuse and cast out of living hell on earth on the planet earth, and I can pray the those who have passed on that went through slavery, that's why death was freedom for most slaves. Some songs about it They hoped there was a better place than the hell they lived through daily.

Things are not much better, today food, and stamp link cards, for Everyone living in poverty faces tough times. Homeless people in America are being rejected in high numbers.

The number has grown. If I gave half of the homeless people a place to live, someone would still be on the brink of being homeless, it would not change tomorrow cause everyday someone is being evicted from their home. drugs, and Alcohol place a major factor in staying under the curse.

Upon This Rock

2009 I was so full of anger and bitterness, so much had happened to me. I was in church, but the church was not in me.

6

God builds his church, up on a Rock, and the gates of hell shall not prevail against it.

Matthew 16:18 KJV And I say also unto thee, that thou art Peter, and upon this rock I will build my church; and the gates of hell shall not prevail against.

What did Jesus mean upon this rock I built my Church?

This verse is talking about something different. Jesus is saying that though He was rejected by the people, arrested, tried, and found innocent, and then crucified anyway, it would not stop him from building His church. It did not stop me from believing in God. Through my suffering.

He died and rose to complete his mission, so we are the rock, and he is the clay maker, we have, to stand on the strongest, foundation, we have. That is on his word, that one day he is coming back,

The Revelation of the world is about to be judged. Victory is mine said the lord, Open your heart, and your mind too, a peaceful life with Jesus. You will not be judged by the same spirit of hell on earth, you will rest with a peaceful spirit.

Forgiving the world, that we live in and the sins of the parents, that have held on to the curse, as long as man has been on earth the curse of the devil.

He wants to win. By showing us everything, he owns in this world, if he can convince you to be miserable, and believe less in God, he will disappear, when you know who he is.

The temptation of material things we want but do not understand, we must not worship them and become filled with greed, and the evil spirit of his world, becoming cold and isolated from God like Satan,

The devil, also referred to as Satan is best known as the personification of evil and the nemesis of good people everywhere. His image and story have evolved over the years, and the devil has been called different names in various cultures, including Beelzebub, lucifer, Satan Baphomet, and Mephistopheles, with various physical descriptions including cloven horns and cloven hooves instead of feet. Gut this malevolent being and his legion of demons continue to strike fear in people as the antithesis of all things good.

The Devil

The devil first showed up in the Bible in the book of Genesis as the serpent who convinced Eve who then convinced Adam to eat the forbidden fruit from the Tree of Knowledge in the Garden of Eden. As the story goes, after Eve fell for the Devil's conniving ways, she and Adam were banished from the Garden of Eden

The Curse Was On Them

And they were doomed to mortality. This is his Kingdom, and he is king over a very wicked world the curse of hell is on earth. And he wants to offer you anything you want but he knows just what your heart desires if it belongs to God then he will temp you and give you the world for your peace of mind, and then, he will have your soul.

Many Christians believe the Devil, was once a beautiful angel, named Lucifer, who defied God and fell from grace. This assumption that he is a fallen angel is often based on the book of Isaiah in the Bible which says, how art thou fallen from

Heaven O Lucifer, son of the morning! How apart thou cut down to the ground which desist weaken the nations.

I often use this statement on my social page Facebook, wake up America you have failed.

What did that mean that it was in 1977 I did not know that America was in trouble, and I was warned.

Let us talk about how we have become who we are today. Not a world where we believe that in God we trust. With so much dying and killing.

Grief is the most natural kind of suffering there Is nothing the hospital or doctor can do.

Elderly people live alone and lonely, some are in pain daily. Sickness, diseases, homelessness, and drugs it like a big play with uncontrollable grown kids playing in hell play grown.

Sometimes we laugh and sometimes we cry but the crying for help never goes away. Knowledge can help us to process some of the things happening to us.

The testimonies of my life and others are too many to write about in this one book. What is the description of hell in many religious cultures? In Christianity and Islam, hell is often depicted as fiery, painful, and harsh. Inflicting suffering on the guilty. Despite these common depictions of hell as a place of fire some portray hell as cold no matter what we will never know because when we die, we want to be back to share with each other.

We worry more about life after, than life right now all life matters and should be treated that way people live in hell right here and now!

WHAT ARE SOME OF THE CHARACTERISTICS OF HELL?

The extreme pain, and environment, conditions, described in the Bible, are not to be interpreted literally. The Bible Descriptions of Hell, Darkest, and Thirsty.

Worms, etc, symbolize symbolizing the emotion of being separated from God.

I never thought that the word Gnashing of teeth meant to anger or upset to show one of his opponents have been gnashing their teeth in with frustration it sounded bad. Some of us live with anger and frustration, daily, but say they are not separated from God.

I find that hard to believe that we would have to go through hell on earth and die and go again.

I hope when you read this, I will clarify my vision of hell on earth my faith in God, and the state of our world today.

I searched Google, it was a tremendous help in authoring my book, in the hope that those who are searching will find some data, and find some comfort in knowing they are not alone.

As a spiritual life coach to save the soul by offering peace, and light in the darkness, of this old hateful world we live in.

I am not saying I can do this, alone, but I wanted to write about it, so you are aware that hell is right here on earth. And to live through it twice, leave questions.

The poor suffer, and the impoverished lack access to proper nutrition, clean water, and sanitation facilities leading to diseases. Malnutrition, infant mortality, and preventable illness remain prevalent issues in impoverished 2022 U.S. Census bureau's report.

37.9 million Americans are considered impoverished... its am a place where greed, crime, corruption, abuse of power, and other problems are widespread in many parts of the world.

Earth, full of hell Lucifer was thrown out of heaven to where?

Earth, there is war, pain suffering, death greed, deception, corruption, murder, backstabbing, liars, false accusations, false witnesses, haters, adulterers, and division, and that sounds about like the description of hell. When you talk to people living on this planet, they will have all sorts of definitions of Hell. And what is it like and do some of us know what it feels like?

Others say hell is unconscious as well as heaven. I call hell the shadows of nature the fear of death, cruelty, resentment, anger, pain, sadness, guilt, shame also money in the shadow, and sexuality, love, and power. And others say Hell is mostly coherently under as Separated, from God, God

In belief, systems with this teaching, God is identified with all goodness and happiness. And love we all know what happens when we wind up in hell, not after death, but during every second of death, we spend the rest of our lives in hell. After when Judged by God have been.

Those cognitive states life without love, joy, warmth, growth, and fulfillment is hell.

Some Asks Are Heaven And Hell On Earth

If you Google its hell is on earth, hell is an area within the district of west Bay, Grand Cayman, its eerie comes from a group of short, black, limestone formations located in the area sinister look is what gave it its infamous name. thanks to google!

I know that hell is a place and location on earth.

Jesus said that hell will be in plane site and the just will walk on the ashes of the wicked when people do all to hades 2 parts paradise, and shoal, the good will be in paradise they will be in shoal.

And then the rapture the good will be taken the bad will stay behind. When judgment is over shoal will be dismantled. There will be a lake of fire on earth. The people in the shoal will be thrown into the lake of fire and will be on earth.

Shoal in the Hebrew Bible is described as an underworld, worse such as descend, deep, and beneath are commonly used when speaking about the Shoal. The Book of Job describes it as the far- thest place possible from Heaven, where the dead go regardless of who they were in their earthly life.

North Korea Says Actually It Is America That Is Living Hell. Written By The Atlantic Global

The U.S. is a living hell!

Now that we know that hell is a place that does not choose race are gender, it will choose the dark soul, that is empty and has no peace, therefore we keep searching to find the other half of your soulmate to make you whole.

You, will not find it outside of you nether, will you find God outside of you. outside of you, everything is inside of you, you were born if you were born with an evil curse on your life.

My Vision Comes True.

In 1977 I was on my way to Honolulu Hawaii on the plane had a though: Wake up America, you have failed, I, quickly wrote the message, on paper then I asked myself, why did I have that thought, safe in America I live in a country we were working, our country was prosperous and I was flying to a job with a contract I had lived in the beautiful city of Hollywood for two years before going to Hawaii.

I believe that God has given me a gift, that is special I can see into my future, not all of it.

I was living in Hollywood Cal at the time of waking up! or was I ever, sleep or did I have a vision?

I was standing behind a tall building with a rooftop restaurant that looked like it was revolving the light was beautiful. I stood on the sand looking at the beautiful ocean miles away I had never seen before. I had no idea where I was.

But this beautiful place stays in my mind I woke up in the middle of the night and explained it to my boyfriend who was sleeping next to me. We let it go. Later, that year I was offered a job in Hawaii. I took the job now even thinking about the vision I had earlier. But the reality of this vision was coming to past I accepted the offer and was on my way.

The pay was good, it was just me, and no one had made decisions for me since I was sixteen years old.

I landed on the beautiful Island of Honolulu, Hawaii!

After a week, I stood in the same spot that I stood in 8 months ago in Hollywood in my bedroom. I saw the tall building with a rooftop revolving restaurant also to the sky the beautiful dark sky with white glittering stars so bright it reflected on the ocean. The sand was white, and the water was blue. I have been here before wow!

But what did that mean, I had taken a walk downtown Waikiki and ended up behind the Waikiki Hilton, where Tina Turner per-formed, I took a walk with this handsome young Soldier. His name was Lee. He was a dark-skinned man, He was not in my dream, but he heard my story, and he came to see me perform, he was inter-ested we talked and exchanged information, he was however, puz-zled about the vision, I had before I came to, to this Island.

But he just smiled he had the whitest teeth I had ever seen and the smoothest dark skin. He was handsome, I did not know he would become my shining knight in Armor.

The following months were fun, I loved the old town, I lived close to the Police station I felt safe and the views I had were beautiful some even, breathtaking. But it would be a sad day for me I would have died if they had not operated on me.

Months passed, and everything worked I saw things and people of all races, not may blacks but brown, and Japanese people the Island natives I was still seeing Lee he was a friend we had met in the place I had envisioned before in the sand. Lee was nice to me, he was engaged back on the mainland; he was stationed on this island, and he needed a friend.

Lee was from California. He showed me around the island and showed me the twin peek the japs flew an attack on Pearl Harbor.

We ate out a lot and had fun Lee was sent to protect me as a gentleman and a Sargent in the United States Army.

He came to see my performance that night I did not show up.

He returned the following night and asked about me and was told I had been taken to the hospital Straub hospital in Honolulu.

I do not remember, going there in an ambulance when I woke up it was dark in the room there was this man whom I through to be my father, turns out to be.

My friend Lee, God had plans for this to happen when I thought he had me locked in hell and that I would die in hell. But he lost that soul he thought he had.

I Recovered and thanked my Agent I spent the rest of my time living by the ocean, but it was time to go, and we both knew we had completed an assignment and a chapter in our lives we would never repeat together again. I had never been on an island before, I was excited to visit, different places, this was where the Japanese flew in and bombed pearl Harbor. The location was called twin peek. I named it the Island of blood because they came through an opening, that gave them access to attack the United Navy at Pearl Harbor one of the bloodiest battles on US soil.

Hell on earth for those left to live with the aftereffects of the storm, the lives that were taken in war The weak lived. They grew stronger from their pain. They had to make better plans to keep this from happening again. As I said pain is definitely a teacher. Life lessons have taught us to make better decisions and wise choices.

Not everyone has to go through pain, but there are so many of us that it is the only life we know. I can only tell you what I know and have heard about living hell on earth in the present!

Losing faith in your leaders we lose hope, in our country, people are losing faith everywhere in leadership, and Governments are rulers all over the world! I am not trying to rewrite everything, in the news and world reports,

I believe the Revelation of time has come! And there is no explanation for why so many of us must live in torment at some point until we die.

Why the poor people are homeless, why did so many doctors write so many prescriptions, and why did the insurance companies pay for it through government funding Medicare?

Drugs that never get rid of the problem, but you must take it your body is addicted to the pain and now they suffer more because of the side effects of the drugs,

This is greed, on behalf of those that are evil and prey on the weaker person to come along.

Overdosing that that just give up living hell on earth.

Suicide: is the one unforgiving sin or is it they wanted die to cause they could not live with the pain it was too great is would never stop this was the only way out.

Will they go to hell or haven? they know hell is real on earth and they found a way to escape?

Since our country is so big on Christianity: we have neglected to see the deep hole in our world that cannot be mended.

Hell, just landed at the front gates of our world. and life just got hotter, Welcome to hell on earth is a nightmare for some of us. I have felt and tried to take my own life, but it was not mine to take it went unreported.

Let Us Look At A Brief Description Of What The Bible Said About Suicide.

Suicide is a tragic reality in our falling world. People experience desperation to the point that they believe the best option is to end their own life it is heartbreaking to lose a loved one to suicide it prompts, a range of questions and a special kind of grief.

But they offer hope- both to those who are considering suicide and to those who have been affected by the suicide of another.

Please understand that suicide is not the best option. For the sake of clarity, should state that suicide is a sin against God and others. However, suicide does not determine a person's eternal destiny our eternal destiny rests solely on God's grace.

Those who trust in Jesus Christ are fully forgiven of every sin and they receive eternal life. Those who reject him remain condemned John 3:16-18-36 Ephesians 2:1-10 If you are considering suicide, please seek help now in the Us, please call 988 0r call 800-

16

2378255 national hotline are please go to a hospital or call 911 alert someone whatever it takes, to get help, you should live and not die.

You will no longer remain a prison of your own mind. To wake up is beautiful I did because wanted to kill myself, and tired a couple of times but because I believe in a God that gave me hope and made me strong.

JOBE WAS TESTED!

I believe when I was born the devil asked God to test me and God allowed him to torment me starting at birth.

Born into this life with nothing but hope Sunflower Mississippi

1951 I am sure it was dark and bleak because we had no money and soon my father would leave my mother, to take care of his four children at the time.

Living in hell on earth, feels something like this! I become cold as the world I live in I feel lost.

Hell is a dark place on earth, nineteen years of waiting for this day to come. To author this book, I hope that someone would understand.

In 1968 I left the state of Illinois and ran away from home I married a boy from Mississippi I should have known I was leaving with the devil. a The life of abuse I once saw as a child I was reliving the abuse, the fighting and drinking things I had seen early in my childhood.

After my mom and dad reunited in together and joined the church together everything changed.

Sad to say but it is here, The Revelation of the world we live in. Just might end!

The News headlines read from N News-break National Headlines North Korean leader commands his country to prepare for war with the United States News break Biden Warns US Military May get pull into Direct conflict with Russia. These kinds of News reports are the norm in our world today.

We live in fear of the end of time, we are lost: Because we are always looking for the perfect life, during our search, we find out that everything comes with a price, and sometimes the price is too high to pay we give up because we are not strong enough and hell may have captured our soul.

The news and our world today! God bless the children. the world Israel was attacked by the Hamas terrorist organization became a threat to our world Israel is at war! In the holy land war killing

War takes the strongest fighters and leaves the weaker ones to become stronger. So that he might have competition with him. An example of weakness in a Physical stage, of weakness Link back to the time when I went in to sweep, the bathroom, floor. I stopped, bent down, got up, and grabbed the wall I thought I could feel a weakness in the wall it was a hollow spot in the picture frame

The picture has no backboard, it was weak my grip was stronger than the picture because the picture hanging on the wall looked strong, but it was Missing some of the backboard had a hollow in the picture cover only the wall could see it. So, there are some things we can only imagine.

So evil is strong in this world, and we have become weak, how can we fight the battle, against evil without faith in God? And paying a price. We are not trusting in God as noted on the back of our us currency. Our Democracy in this country has overall gotten weaker.

The Storyline Of Peter-Pan.

At some point, all adults believe that fairytales **are not real.** the tv series was based on this young boy, Peter was a dreamer. Most of the younger generation may not have ever heard of Peter Pan.

Peter Pan was around the age of twelve, that was my guess. His mission was to take the boys to a land called Neverland, where there were no rules, for children just food, and play, in his imagination he was strong enough to fly in the windows of people's homes and take the children with him to play. All children love to play in a make-believe world!

However, we must wake up in the story the boy Peter gives in to his weakness, and the stronger fighter has arrived and is willing, to train the weaker one that still wants, to play and live in a world with no rules.

When Peter grew up, he woke! and realized that everything comes at a price!

America is facing this dooms day warning! and it will come with a price.

America has an Election coming up in 2024 and we have a ex-President that has been.

Indicted so many times I stop counting he is encouraging negatively to grow! He feeds off hate, he loves only himself.

As an African America woman, I would never vote for him. He is trouble.

His, evil mind of self only has contributed to America politics becoming a joke, and other countries and world leaders are making jokes about the election and hoping that They too can destroy America.

These words he uses witch hunt and make America great again when the white people own slaves.

The ex-President of the united is a danger to his own health.

His mind does not seem quite right, his heart is evil if the President does not respect his country and is accused of disrespecting our leader in the Military, calling them bad name bad names, and saying they would be put to death which is evil. Sending them to be in prison for life. And publicly making fun of our disabled veteran.

To me, a man, that does not respect his country does not have a home in his country. But he wants to Make America great again!

Remember that the strongest of evil comes to destroy those that are weaker.

Today people have little faith in our Presidential choices, people have no interest in the Presidential candidates therefore weakening our world.

As an Apostolic woman, I grew up believing, that everything, does, come, with a price. In life, we must accept that we do not know what we want, and until we do, we will never find the right person to lead our country but for now we just do not care.

Let Us.

Look at a brief description of was the bible says about suicide as a tragic reality in our fallen world. That people experience desperation to the point that they believe the best option is to end their own lives is heartbreaking. To lose a loved one to suicide prompts a range of questions and a special kind of grief. But the bible offers hope-both to those who are considering suicide and to those who have been affected by the suicide of another.

Please understand that suicide is not the best option.

For the sake of clarity, we should state that suicide is a sin against God and others. However, suicide does not determine a person's eternal destiny our eternal destiny rests solely on God's grace, those who trust in Jesus Christ are fully forgiven of every sin, and they receive eternal life; those who reject him remain condemned John 3:16 –18-36 Ephesians 2:1-10

If you are anyone you know may be considering suicide, please seek help now in the US, please call 988 or Call the 1-800-237-8255 national hotline go to a hospital or call 911 to alert someone whatever it takes to get help you should not die but live.

You will no longer remain a prison to your own mind to wake up is beautiful, I did because I wanted to die and tried three times.

But I had hoped to live and not die I alerted someone God, and he gave me hope, I forgave myself for the thoughts and I lived on to be strong and you shall live on to be strong. This is the second book I live to write. Someone who must suffer, with pain, every day is hell on earth.

Mental Illness

Personality disorders are few but there are more have always been amazed and a faithful reader of Psychology today! The minds of those who work, and study, the field of psychology, especially those who have contributed time and study to provide us with safer, treatment to the sickness of the brain.

They have made tremendous progress in the field of mental health.

My sister Dr. Evelyn Chenier broke the Poverty curse in her family by becoming a doctor she has inspired me with her purpose and has helped so many in the communities Dr. Evelyn born in poverty she is a licensed Mental health Counselor -LPC, PHC, MS, NBCC, NCC she Study and received her degrees at the Nation Louis University, where developed a deep understanding of the complex social and psychological dynamics that impact individuals and communities

She broke the curse to be the first of the 12 children in my family she broke the curse of poverty over her family. Also, my Aunt, my father's sister, was the first in my father's family that I am aware of to also succeed in breaking the curse of poverty and education. Dr.

Virginia Caples, 1946, from Doddsville Miss, held numerous leadership positions throughout her life. The first female interim President of Alabama A&M University in Normal, Alabama, her career began at Alcorn State university in 1976 she continued her education at Iowa State University where she received her M.A. and PH.D. There are a lot more accomplishments these two have achieved.

We experienced some of the hardest times, back then. But we survived the injustice of life at the hand of the evil spirit of Jim Crow the devil. On earth my mom worked the fields were my ancestors as slaves, spent all their lives in hell on earth they paid the price to the tree of life, in another world. A better world, a free world.

I was visiting a local thrift store. I like to buy used books. I used to like reading, but my eyes and attention span have limited time to read, oh and everyday life responsibilities.

I found a book for $2.99 I right away took an interest in this book because it suggested that we should treat mental illness just like any other sickness.

The end of mental illness, the end of mental illness was a book I was interested in.

DR. Amen explain why you no longer must rely solely on standard, treatment offered by experts trained according to and old Pro paradigm while medication and talk therapy, are sometimes helpful and appareled, there is much we can do to improve your own brain health and increased practitioners are using evidence-based neuroscience.

The mental five hopes that we are on the cusp of a while-need paradigm of treating issues like depression, anxiety ADHD, bipolar, personality disorders, and even schizophrenia.

Explain why standard treatment may not have helped you or a loved one be healed or truly healed for the long term.

Teach you how to contribute to your own brain healing and prevent or reverse the problems that are stealing your mind.

Show you how to keep healthy or rescue it if it is headed toward a dark place. We have considered how many children were born with mental illness, that goes untreated.

Because of the faith and beliefs and generation **curses.**

To be rejected by a world that tells you, you are unfit to live in this world mentally. But they have no place for you to go. Treatment is a life of pills and rejection, fears of the unknown, put aside to live in a world where you are called and look crazy.

Mental illness is hell on earth for some of us. Is a death sentence like cancer. It is a sickness that we treat with fear.

MENTAL ILLNESS

Mood and anxiety disorder, ADHD addiction, PTS. psychosis personality disorders there in much more in the world than loss of how to help each other by expecting your own responsibility it is the only way you can help to show action to repair your damage and believe in what you see only never give up on your dreams if you do you give up and world has never known you because you just drop off the globe

Look at why we should open our minds to the possibility of respecting mental health the same as any other sickness.

Pain on the left of the number highest number 98% will say pain is painful and torture too much to bear sometimes we give in, and we give up and become dependent on something or someone else cause we rejected and gave up on ourselves, I will not give up. Life is a battlefield. I am always in battle with myself to keep my peace. I was the answer to my happiness. I was searching in the wrong places for my sadness because I did not realize that my sadness and my happiness were in me. I had to accept them it was too late for a retake of life. And those feelings and mistakes remain on my record to be judged by a higher court, in the kingdom of God.

Hell on earth has been descried as being born with a biblical curse.

Chronic Stress Ruling Our Lives

Let us look at why we should open our minds to the possibility of respecting mental health the same as any other sickness.

Pain on the level of numbers is the highest number and 98% will say pain is painful and torture too much to bear sometimes we give in and we give up and become depend on something or someone else cause we rejected and gave up on ourselves.

I will not give up it's a battlefield, and I am always in battle with myself to keep my peace.

I am the answer to my happiness and my sadness. Today I realized my mistakes and I accepted them, there was no retake my final mistake would remain on my record to be judged by a higher court and Kingdom.

America, the harlot that was in bed with the world, has been discovered and now has a new dictator. They trust them to speak about their evil and hate, with negative behavior toward humankind.

I have family members who have lived and died with mental illness and there was nothing I could have done to save them.

Because I was always told by the Apostolic women that you must have a sound mind to be helped.

I believe people who have untreated mental illness are living hell on earth.

Now there is more data out here you can find on Google and other websites.

These are some of the major points that impeded, understanding that because of parent's choices, sin really, does fall on the parent. This has been the biggest problem with families today.

Breaking the bond of father and son supported data shows children from fatherless homes are more likely to become poor, become involved in drug and alcohol abuse, and drop out of school and suffer from health and emotional problems.

The Consequences of Fatherless National center for fathering.

AFPI Fatherhood and crime May 25, 2023, there are over 18 million fatherless children in the us. Fathers are absent. Approximately 80% of single-parent households in any nation in the world

Fatherless families are more likely to live in poverty than married-couple families. Fatherless children are more likely to delinquent behavior.

Father absence as a predictor of violence is robust for both male and female violence 70% of juveniles in state-operated institutions come from single-parent homes.

Individuals from father-absent homes are 279% more likely to carry guns and deal drugs than their peers.

Most adolescents who enter the justice system have suffered from parental abandonment, substance abuse, or dysfunctional households.

In the study of 75 juvenile delinquents, 66% experienced father-less, 20% had never lived with their father and 25% had an alcoholic father.

It has been reported that fatherless children are anywhere from 3 to 20 times more likely to be incarcerated than children raised in dual-parent households.

71% of teachers and 90 % of law enforcement officials state that the lack of parental supervision at home is a major factor that contributes to violence in a study of 56 school shootings, only 10 of the shooters (18%) were raised in a stable home with both biological parents. 82% grew up in either an unstable family environment or grew up without both biological parents together.

This is hell on earth! That comes with everyday storms of life when the curse is on you. And your children, children to repeat the cycle The sins of the parent do fall on the children.

The Facts Of Fatherless

Some data suggests that 72% of adolescent murders and 70 percent of long-term prison inmates come from fatherless homes. Children who feel closeness to their father are 80% less likely to spend time in jail and the list will go on.

I am seventy-two years old today! I have moved on thanks to the Pastors and Apostolic women and men teaching me how to love and forgive.

That saved my life. I listened a little late, but I grew up in the faith I had to rest I have been to a lot of places, and I have more stories than you will care to read.

My life has been mostly sad born in poverty, with family, sickness, and everyday situations, that come with this kind of lifestyle. Life has been real. I trust you will stop and think about the hell you may not have been born in but created it. Change it today repent. We shall live and not die.

Life will always be challenging and fun you must live the best life you can. And find your peace, to have been a free soul. Without living in fear.

A Biblical, Standpoint Definition Of Hell Is A Place.

Not everyone can relate to pain, which brings shame, and a guilty feeling of loneness. You once felt love, and passion you no longer feel that.

Your dreams, have disappointed you and you no longer have that passion.

You were sent to hell, on planet earth. Increasingly, darkness is all around. There is and there never was any promise to grant you a better life.

This is your battle, a curse to fight for your chance to make, wrong into right.

But you were born for this, this is your life! on planet Hell ON EARTH!

A place that has taken on more passengers, every day.

The world you were born in has sent many new souls to live in this world of hell. On earth, our minds are deteriorating as we fight the impossible dream. We have lived our lives the way it has been given.

We have blamed ourselves for things we could never have changed. You tried but you did not know how to change your Never give up on your soul you will have it for eternity.

Praying to be taken out of this world but afraid of dying and not existing. Forever.

Find your purpose and service do not misplace your purpose.

You have been judged by the torment, sleepless nights, pain, misuse, abuse, sexual assault shame, and blame you are walking through life dead. Satan's wishes have been granted because you have lost faith in yourself and your ability to continue the dream you had. Someone stole your dream. Darkness, lies, and secrets have a special place. It is the beginning of destruction hiding from the world always tells the truth.

I lied and daydreamed so much as a child to blotch out my child-hood life rape and abuse. I covered up my pain until I was confused as an adult about what was real and what was not.

From my book Storms of Life Why I became a life Coach to save lives and souls. By adjusting, to modifying the problem, erasing the negative mindset, of the brain, and rethinking it as the brain moves, forward, letting go of limited beliefs.

Making the necessary changes for a more spiritual life and natural life. Excepting, what you cannot change, and changing, what you can.

Which was ridiculously hard for me to do, in my case and situation.

I was born in this place. I have deemed this earth hell on earth because of the suffering related to what hell would be like according to the king James version.

An eternal suffering, cursed upon families and friends, their stories, of their abuse and pain that passed on from one generation to the next, we live in fear, of the unknown and the possibility of never healing, daily pain is hell. Poverty is an embarrassment to the poor. We were born into this world by our judgment of what we would become and what our lives would be like with no say.

It was a judgment of a life of poverty, sickness, and death.

Our storms will never end. There will always be unexpected storms in life. However, we can help, make a better world, and end the feeling of being doomed dreams cursed at birth for some of us.

Especially for some of us who are living a nightmare waiting to wake up. But you are not sleeping, your thinking is stinking wake-up. You must realize this is your life and you fail to believe in yourself. Ask God to remove the curse and be on your way you are forgiven.

We can only hope for today, be excited about today! And dream about tomorrow.

Until we feel we can multitask this would not be good advice to worry and plan for tomorrow. We all hope for tomorrow. And we plan days and months, sometimes, years to be disappointed especially concerning our children.

Hollywood

Hollywood was beautiful, back in 1972 when I lived there. Today it is full of drug addicts, people walking around with no hope, no brain, the walking dead.

Accepting defeat. I know all about it.

1971, I was there looking for the dream, the American dream I was disappointed then and today I find it hard to believe that Americans have dropped so low for not accepting our defeat and changing the way we see ourselves not what Hollywood sees. Are we doomed has evil doers, suck the life out of their victims and they are living in some kind of hell on earth in their minds.

The ex-President of the United States of America! charge with a crime, encouraging Americans to break in and threaten people's lives. People, threatening to hang the Vice President.

Our world is coming to that end no one believes in the American dream anymore. Doctor King's dreams come true, all of God's children are free.

Revelation. has been a fact check the book I have written is the revelation in my life I was born in hell on earth!

In the last 44 years, I have watched American fail and now she knows the truth, she must except her defeat, she has become more or less of a country you can believe in.

An over-stimulated word that promises the American dream that no longer exists for some of us.

Man has always face challenges, and as far back as I can remember are cared to remember.

Are we at the closing of the book of revelation?

I was given this message to write by a supernatural being. My time is running out. Over fifty years with no clue how to author a book in 2009 I started writing about my life so full of pain it took me all that time to obey the calling.

There is something in this book that draws us right to the end of time. Excepting the reality of how we have to understand

We can repent and leave this world knowing our souls will live in peace forever in peace or leave our souls here searching for a peace you will never find the earth will burn up the wars of fires will clash into the earth and the whole word will be on firer and he will come like a thief in the night 2 Peter 3:10 KJV but the days of the lord will come like a thief in the night.

The bible verse says the earth will be destroyed by fire.

He will come again, like a thief the heavens will disappear with a roar, the elements will be destroyed by fire, and the earth and everything in it will be laid bare.

Why me? Why was I given my assignments on earth I was born to serve?

I recall reading about so many that sea took housing for so many who gave their life to the sea. To be free of this including slavery, and the many wars, shipwrecks, and plane crashes we somehow must pay a price. To live forever in peace Jesus died he paid the price for our sins. And not you will pay for the injustice you have inflicted on God's children.

I remember an old movie a few years ago on tv once upon a time. A storybook movies and Fairytales

Peter pan as he got older in the movie, he knew.

Everything comes would come with a price

American history gives us enough information about the evil and cruel world we have helped recreate.

The evil-doer is entering a doomsday of suffering.

Hell on earth will end for some of us heaven and earth shall not pass away. But right now, hell is present.

That day the storms blew in at the gates of hell. Wake up America you have failed.

War gave death to the brave and left the weaker to defend against themselves.

Because all the brave men who were killed or wounded in this country have lived decades without war.

We must begin to dream again of the place in our mind where we would like to be with our families and friends and what kind of place it would be.

For me, I would like to have found a perfect husband, for me and only me and my children who would have no worries, no abuse or sickness.

My dream would be for peace, love, and respect for ourselves and others.

My world would not include wars, killings of babies, and little children like a cold-blooded animal.

There are so many waiting in line for a perfect life, a copied life. And nothing is real but the dream you are chasing.

With a world in the misfits of all its darkness.

Leaving planet hell on earth is a dream Wake up! 10/07/2023 Hamas was between two countries Gaza and Israel at War! Blood has been shared.

Killing over 3000 children it was reported. Last month there was an update.

Hell on earth just landed at the Gates of hell.

CRONIC STRESS RULING OUR LIVE

Sickness. Pain on the level of the number the highest number and 98% will say pain is painful and torture too much to bear sometimes we give in, and we give up and become depended on something or someone else when they reject us, we gave up on ourselves I will not give up its a battlefield of the mine the spiritual mind.

I was born on the battlefield with myself to keep my peace. I am the answer to my own happiness and my own sadness, and today I realize my mistakes.

I have accepted them. There are no retakes. My final mistake would remain on my record to be judged by a higher court, and kingdom.

America, the magnificent that goes in bed with other countries now our world has been discovered and now we

Have a new dictator. They trust him to speak about their evil doings, their hate, and their negative behavior toward humankind. God children

To be rejected by a world that tells you that you are unfit to live in it mentally but has no place for you to go cast out.

The treatment leaves us with a life-filled will rejection, and fears, of the unknown put aside to live in a world where you are called crazy is a location on earth in the mind called hell on earth.

Mental illness is hell on earth for some of us. A death sentence like cancer. It is a sickness. But we treat it with fear.

I had family with some kind of mental illness and until you are treated with medications to fix it I never will we have except those that have the illness and understand to love and be kind. Not fearful and reject them because they are different from others. It will become hell on earth if a mentally ill person gets addicted to drugs, their life and yours would be hell on earth. They are tormented. They are living their life in hell on earth.

The Shape Our World Is In Today!

Israel-Hamas war torturing, men women, and children daily. The fear of death is powerful if only for a minute.

These behaviors of war are made by leaders, but to me it is like children, playing a game of chess checkmate will put our world at risk like children playing in a playground with no adult around. But our father in heaven is protecting us from ourselves, we will destroy the life taken away from the children which is called death.

Fathers are absent from the home and mothers find it hard to raise young boys. They are hearing disrespectful comments coming from their sons because of their anger toward their fathers.

They have caused many problems for the mother to work and pay bills, and deal with courts, and police. Their disappointment has turned integrand they are not at peace with a life of unexpected situations that happen daily in the home of a single mother raising boys to be men.

Sometimes suffering from homelessness, hunger, pain, and suffering. Without a father.

Rejected by your own father, breaking the bond of father and son. Feeling lost

The feeling of being unwanted when you did nothing is made until after the application date."

A young person with no understanding of why this happens to him is painful, and some will turn to drugs to ease the pain. kill the pain, some become addicted forever, living in a place of darkness.

36

Our country was attacked by our own citizens our president has been indicated for insurrection on the Capitol White house for a day the fear of Americans was at the highest level and things have been worse.

I Shared in my book storms about my life, and so many other cases, like mine if you are at this stage in your life and are reading this book ease up trust, and believe that hell is here right now< not in the after world this is the afterworld for now!

2020 was ruff remembering Covid millions of lives we lost. Love one's hearts were broken losing a mother, sister brother, aunts, uncles, cousins, nephews' grandparents, friends, and neighbors.

This was the first time I can ever remember the house of Worship was shut down. Fear gripped our world, the storms blew.

And yet we hear some stories, about abuse, rape, and false accused, in prison children are rap including boys.

Family missing for a year. Nature has claimed its share of taking too many lives.

The torment and punishment are overwhelming, especially in the elderly.

Knocking On Death's Door Living By Faith

After the birth of my second daughter, I started bleeding a lot. I was diagnosed with tumors on the ovary before I had a DNC scraping of the wound, I suffered so much that I had blood clots and lots of pain.

The Devil tried to kill me!

My suffering just of my body happened in Chicago the hospital St Marry in Chicago, Illinois 1986

My two daughters and my husband live in Roger Park, Illinois. It has been forty years since that day, and I will never forget it.

This is what happened to me that morning I got the girls off two schools they were babies, my oldest was eight and my youngest daughter, was four-year-old she was in day care.

Afterward, I went to my appointment to see Dr. Miller his office was off Howard Street an old white man; I trusted him I had been to his off a few times.

I had no ideal this man was about to try and kill me.

I walked in and walked out feeling that I would be better. He gave me a prescription to stop bleeding. I picked up the strip it was a blood thinner

And went home to feed my daughters, took the medication, laid down, and woke up in a pool of blood-soaked, the per-medic drove me to the hospital the next day I woke up with pain and gas. The nurses told me to walk I would feel better I felt like hell.

That did not release the pain later that same night I awoke with tubs in my nose and mouth what is going on I through. I was bleeding Inside again like when I was in Hawaii, I hurt so bad. But they assured me I would be ok.

The next week I was still there for two operations, and it was not over the third operation did it. They placed in me the ICU for months.

I have no idea how long I was there. I was so weak. I was bandaged up from head to toe. Was I dying?

No one could visit long after I came out of the operation.

They put me in a private room. my husband and my sister, Johnnie were visiting at the time I saw the nurses rush into the room shock me twice, and call code blue I was dying bleeding so fast that they rushed me to the operation room I looked back, and my bed was soaked with my blood, for the last time on my way there I was ice cold I got off in the hallway on my way to the operating room I got off the cart and walk alongside my body I could see the doctors, in white coats and nursing in blue and white uniforms was this real I was out of my body.

I found out that Dr. Miller had given me blood thinner no recorder they had to operate like in Hawaii.

Upon my arrival at the hospital, they tried to reach my doctor. He was on vacation out of the country. I had so many blood transfusions I was isolated because back then blood transfusions could have transmitted Aids to my blood.

This new doctor wan from Indian who saved my natural body, God saved my spiritual life.

Because I was sent to a Pastor, in Chicago by my parents Pastor in Waukegan. He was one of the nicest white men I had ever met both him and his wife. They were at the hospital every time I woke up when I was in ICU.

They had a son and a daughter, The Pastor loved to hear me sing the song Jesus. In fact, about three or four years ago he asked me to come and sing that song his wife had passed. And he was remarried, it was not the same. But his love was.

He died a year later. The whole time I was there even if I could not interact with prayer, they came to the hospital often and prayed for me my family lives about an hour's drive from Chicago.

So they did not come to the hospital that much my sister Johnnie stayed home with the girls because my husband had a job.

It was difficult for her with one hand, but she did it with a smile on her face. The nightmare started.

When I was a child, I used to have nightmares, of a bear chasing me into a hole. After, even as an adult, I had nightmares about police chasing me into a dark cave I would get away but always woke us from the nightmare shaking with fear. I believe the devil started to chase me and kept on through my drinking and bad behaviors he did not want me to write this book I lived in his hell, anger, and bitterness, most of my young life, fighting and running from him, I was trying to outrun the devil when he knew that wherever I ended up he finds me and he aways did.

During my Stay in the hospital, everything was not clear to me every detail of what happened to me.

My new doctor, that God appointed to help save my life.

His name was Doctor Majida he was not an American with dark skin but not black he was from India. Soft-spoken and concerned.

My stay was long I went to the hospital around November just before Thanksgiving. I was discharged just before Valentine's Day. About three months the longest ever away from my babies.

One day I awoke and was shocked by the amount of time I was there. I slept a lot I was on a breathing machine feeding machine three blood transfusions and three operations trying to correct the bleeding.

Dr Majida was kind and he let me know the God I knew had saved my life it was hard for him, but he obeyed and saved my life he was chosen.

I was told there were thirteen chief-of-staff doctors working on my case.

In my dream every night it was raining hard, and I was again running, I ran, and the blood bubbles would case me out in the rain every night and then they would burst, and blood would cover the ground it was all over my body for a month it was always raining and dark.

I spoke to my mom about my dream of her being a true apostolic woman of God a praying woman she would know. She assures me that the blook was the blood of Jesus and the water the rain was the spiritual side of my being.

Fighting to take my life was the evil side run, run, as fast as you can from God he was always there even after the spirit had visited he never left this was his kingdom and he was here to do his job to win the soul for his kingdom of doom! But he lost my soul that he thought he had I have had enough of your world and it's been hell on earth I am so glad it didn't last forever. After my children but the battle is over Jesus took over and now the promise is for me and my children, and their children, children's. A doctor in a sick room is a healer of the soul.

I was discharged, weighed about 96 pounds walked with kin, and was very weak, but I lived. I was full of the spirit that I would soon leave again, and I was back in hell again fighting for this day to author this book. I was called to the battlefield to fight. I have everlasting peace because I receive it here in my mind and it will be the only thing, I take with me in my peace forever. I am thankful as a child because we were so poor, I would get the younger children and sometimes my older sisters would sit in and join in laughing and joking about revering the role of white and black if not but an hour we had that, but the richness of the world was not what I was searching for I was looking for love peace, and happiness, all in the wrong places.

A forty-year-old profit came true. I was here on the 31st when my life started at age sixteen when a voice spoke to me and said I would be back. I thought once I was out of her, I would never come back. There is a season for all things. This is my new season, and I am peaceful.

Dr. Miller finally had his justice he made a mistake that killed a woman under his care I do not have the details, but I heard that his medical license was revoted, But I was free, for whatever reason this happened he would receive his punishment for his evildoing are his human mistake, but he messes with God choose servant.

This was the third time; the devil tried to kill me. The time my car was hit by a train one early evening I left Chicago to visit a friend who was stationed at Fort Sheridan Illinois Army base.

They were a no-show so I started drinking ended up crying and getting stuck in the railroad tracks there was a sign close detour go back I was all in my feelings and the devil knew it, I was crying so hard, and it was raining yes here he was again chasing me in the rain.

It was dark I saw the light on the train I froze but something happened and I was rushed out of the car on the passenger side I for some reason was not thinking I opened the trunk to get my daughter's school clothes I don't how I sober up but when the police came to the train conductor said he saw the car and was too close to stop how could anyone get out they was looking to see a bloodied mess. It was a spiritual moment and an angel rescued me. And again, you miss that soul you thought you had. Devil angel of the pits from hell. They called my husband, and he came to the front end of the car which was about a mile away from where I was hit. I took a DUI, I passed, and I went home sober.

In the closing of my book rather you read the entire book it's real you will understand I played the cards I was given I did my best with what I had I was thankful because I knew that there were others who would love to be in my shoes

Someone is always worse off than you. I pray daily that our children will understand we were not meant to live in hell on earth we were supposed to be living a clean Godley life and grow in goodness and be happy, but the devil is the dream stealer. Peace on earth once again, or hell on earth you will lift your eyes, you will be home.

HELL ON Earth

Johnnie Red

An unexpected storm that would change our life forever. apostolic women don't play we pray.

It was not always that way for Johnnie she had a family.

They were poor but shared the one thing their mother believed in, Praying.

Bleeding in her brain caused her to lose her mobility and speech at the time she was confined to a wheelchair. And sent home a year later to her husband and her baby boy. Her, faith, and independence. Grace, and Integrity, humble as pie, inspire, me to write about her testimonies. She deserves it she was not alone she had her family to come home.

Beautiful light brown eyes. My sister johnnie made friends, easy. But we are always careful about who she would make friends with the upped kids, their families, had money.

My sister, Johnnie, was born on June 9th, 1947. I was born four years later, on her birthday. We became twins, because of the date of our birthday. We would share birthdays forever.

Jr. High in Dodgeville Mississippi.

My sister Johnnie was lucky she was picked to live with our grandfather my dad's dad he had money, land, and respect in his

43

community. She was happy a light-skinned Black girl. In the South, a favorite among the dark-skinned men, this was the normal in the South.

Johnnie was very popular

After moving to Illinois, she had beautiful friends, they had nice clothes, Bea my second oldest sister, were close in age,

They spent time together, with the same friends. When they left, they promised to come back for us.

My Sister Johnnie laughed and partied she had lots of fun dating. She found the man of her dreams and married him. My sister Johnnie had one son.

Here are the storms, they blew into my sister Johnnie. Life and change her life forever.

Around 1975. She was rushed to the hospital from work and hell knocked on Johnnie's door.

I received the news that my sister Johnnie was sick, but I lived in California, at that time, and would come home as soon as possible.

When I, got there I did not believe what I saw, this was not my beautiful sister, who was this I walked into the room and would be in shock if you could have seen, the look on my face of shock as tears rushed to my eyes.

She called my name, but her words were not clear.

Her head was in a wrap. It was swollen, and unrecognized, i was in the wrong room. Did anyone pray for her? pretty sister.

She was in a wheelchair, and that broke my heart, I asked why would God let her come here like this.

Once I got home, I was not feeling well I was throwing up blood I was rushed to the same hospital with Johnnie, across the hall from Johnnie's room.

When I was better, I visited her room, and I was able to push her I pushed her around in a wheelchair.

I talked to her knowing she did not understand any thing that was going on.

As I was discharged, I promised her I would see her again. She had to go to Chicago, for rehabilitation.

I did not come back until around 1978. Around September, I was with my first child, and I came to Johnnie's Apartment, she was there along with her son, who was in first grade. Her husband had left her and her son because she, could not walk she was in a wheel-chair chair with limited movement, she cared for her son, as best as she could he was, out of control, I asked her what had happened to her husband, she starts laughing and crying at the same time What was funny was she laughed at everything, even herself.

My sister was a mess I, stayed with her until my Baby girl, was born in April 1979.

I helped her with her son, but I soon moved out. Years after, in 1986 I had bleeding problems and was in the hospital, my daughters were with their father, he had to work, during the day. My sister, Johnnie, came and stayed for months, caring for my girls. with one hand taking care of an eight-year-old, and a four-year-old until I came home from the hospital four months later, she did what she could for them, with one side of her body disability.

My sister, Johnnie, found a new kind of love. The ones that would love her and never leave her, are, making her feel bad about her disability.

She found Jesus! What happens when she meets Jesus, in a wheelchair? At a small church in Waukegan, Illinois on West Street The year she found a new life with Christ and a new friend that followed Christ. My Mother was her inspiration to come to church and have faith that God, would give her a better life, and he did.

My sister Johnnie soon got out of the wheelchair and walked. She lived by herself until her husband took her son. He remarriage and left her alone. his new life with his new wife.

Her son loved his mom so as soon as he got out of high school,

I was moving away she asked me to take him down south with me. And I did that was my way of paying her back for taking care of my girls.

He moved away met a girl, and created a family year later he got killed away from home in a horrible way.

Johnnie remarried a man in the church who would take care of her and love her, second husband.

Living A Safe Life With God!

Johnnie gave her life to Christ and was happy.

Before she married, she lived with my mom. She had a car, and she drove it. She got an apartment, she was alone, she was in church, and she had friends. She raised her son in church, and she became an usher, in the church she was happy it was hard because her son never took her seriously, he knew she could not get mad, so he made her laugh at him when she needed to whip him, he runs but because of my sister condition, he got away with it.

In 1992 I moved to Anniston, AL. Our father passed away that year.

Her son depended on me a lot since I was in and out of his life

46

a lot.

Her son lived with me. She had prayed that he would be ok. I went back to Alabama to live for the next two years.

Johnnie was a soft-spoken, quiet woman of God.

She was thankful that she could live life without, family and be independent on her own, even with her left side being of no use to her unless she assisted her arm, she dragged the left foot. She would use scissors to open the package and use her teeth to tare a package open.

She loved reading, the bible and she kept notes of everything, her Pastor and the teacher spoke, or read.

She was 100% faithful.

Johnnie moves to Zion, where she lives in a wonderful place, all alone, she went to church that was her life she had no friends but Jesus. That changed once she got married again.

Life changed for Johnnie. I had opened a new help center to help people achieve their goals and I life little that this white man who went to church with my sister was sad and lonely like my sister, he cried out for help. With my compassion, what could I do but help?

I asked him if he knew my sister and he replied we go to church together, your brother's church. Wow! I thought I would introduce them, and I did.

At that time, she could not go on a date alone! They needed a chaperone at 55 years old. So, my mom and I shared their first date. He wanted us to watch his favorite show which was the train show, it was the longest movie ever.

After that, they went on lots of dates, fell in love, and got married. And stayed together until death did them part and he passed.

Johnnie fell and had to live with me, for about two years. We shared sad and happy moments.

One day I asked if she was ready to live on her own, and she said yes. I went online to fill in an application at a senior building.

She moved and stayed there for seven years. She was happy again, and she soon found a caregiver; she needed help doing things that were now hard for her to do.

Before my sister Johnnie moved out of my home, she had a friend that she loved. They went shopping, out to eat, to the movies, and to church together.

One day, she said her friend told her they should not be friends anymore, and she was crushed.

She found a loyal friend in the end, and they are still friends, her name is sister Max.

Johnnie's new friends were older than Johnnie. But full of life she made friends with other sisters from the church, as well Johnnie knew lots of people at church after all her brother was the Pastor, and her mom and entire family went to the same church.

Max was like a sister, she drove, and Johnnie would take her to every family event we had.

They were inseparable. They dress fashionably, and they are showing up at every function.

In the church, there was a prayer team. Going to nursing homes, visiting, and praying. What a fantastic team faith in God had given my sister Johnnie a second chance. To live and to save her soul she was humble and thankful. She was kind and loveable. Her lost, would have been too much for someone else but not Johnnie, faithful and thankful, and never complained about her losses.

Her teenage sweetheart, her first husband, left her

Then the terrible news of her son getting killed, shot in the head at 3:00 am.

She had to go out of town and have him shipped home. She never once lost it. God knew it and fixed it, he brought her through. Along with her family and church family

The saddest day was when her sisters had to come and break the news about the death of her son. Her second husband was by her side, and there he stayed until he died. She had lost her mother and father. and her only son she was not bitter or anger.

She walked with a cane because her left side was paralyzed. she walked, with Jesus and never asked for help.

This is the amazing Road to the end for Johnnie.

In 2023, our sister Bea passed away.

They were close only two years apart when they were growing up.

Our sister had moved out of the state of Illinois, they reconnected, before she passed.

Johnnie loved all her brothers and sisters; she was humble. After the loss of her son, she never returns to his grave site. She said she gave him back to God. She did not speak of him that much, after.

Her second husband had several heart, operations, on his heart, He was placed in a nursing home; she was not able to care for him. Something Strange happened she felt and ended up at the same nursing home, for a month, they were in the same room.

She got out and came to live with me because she had no one. He was relocated close to her. He relocated to a facility in the same town where she lives, She visited for over a year then. One day we received a call saying her husband was not going to make it.

We rushed to the hospital and within an hour he was gone. I stood there In Shock. What would she do, I cried aloud No" I was hurt for my sister.

He loved her so much, they loved each other. They both had been married before, he had no children, and she had one son. But at this moment she had no husband, and no children, or grandchildren. She has lived with me for about two years. Johnnie and I became closer and we were able to talk about some things about her life she was ashamed of she opened up to me, and later was able to talk about them in a group meeting with women from her church. One day I asked Johnnie if she wanted to move out if she was ready. independent as always, she said yes.

I knew she needed her space to pray and be closer to her place of worship.

I found a place in Waukegan near downtown, the lacey apartments. About 10 blocks away from her church. A senior building, that charged according to her income.

It used to be a penthouse close to lake Michigan, the beach was also close. fill out the paperwork, online we viewed the apartment she moved in and remained there until March of 2023

One night during my assignment as her caregiver, and sister, I spent the night.

I had no idea what I was there for. I had no idea she was losing her memory; I took her to the doctor; it was full-blown Dementia. I shopped, cooked, and paid bills for her. Here caregiver had spoken to our family about her medical conditions concerning her mind.

She was left alone all day, six days out of the week, except for the three days a week when the caregiver would be present for four hours, and when she would go to church on Sunday. I had stayed there for about seven months when she fell.

My office was close to her apartment, about a mile or two off the same street in Washington St.

Her new friend was closer to her than a sister. She took her shopping, to church, to eat out, and accompanied her at every family event. Max was there at this time.

One day last year, in 2022, Maxie was at her own birthday party at home, when she went to open the door and had a stroke.

She never returned home. It was like a death because she had no memory of her sister or her friend. They visited a lot of nursing homes together, praying for the sick. They were inseparable.

She would not remember or speak of Max again; she would lose her memory as well. Her friend Max passed this year.

This was a tough time for my beautiful sister Johnnie. She walked slower and became lonely again.

February 3rd, 2023, Johnnie passed out at three a.m. I slept over that night. She looked and acted normal all day, she watched TV and ate a three-course meal for dinner. She loved to eat fried chicken.

She was happy but after the passing of our sister which will be going on two years in February 2025.

She was planning on going to her homegoing. In fact, she packed her bag a week early. I said "Johnnie, are you going somewhere?" she replied "to our sister Beatrice's home going" and my heart stopped. I knew dementia had gotten worse. Much worse.

At night, I was sleeping on the couch when I heard a loud noise, it was Johnnie hitting the floor. She hit her head and passed out.

She would miss her sister going home.

That night, I rushed into the room when she was passed out. She was not responding, her eyes were back in her head and wide open, she clenched her teeth, and I yelled "Johnnie!"

Life would change for Johnnie after that.

She was to move out of her home to move back into my house after she moved out in 2015. Moving back in 2023 was the end of Johnnie's long life of independence. She woke up one morning in the hospital.

Johnnie was diagnosed with Dementia in 2020. She was mostly isolated at home after losing her sister and friend of over twenty years.

She was packing and ready to go without a date or time for our sister's homegoing.

She showered and got dressed on Monday. I would say to her "Hey, where you are going, Johnnie Red?" She would respond "to church." I knew it was not Sunday but she didn't.

I became her caregiver around November 2022

This was my time to see her be happy again. I did everything to make her happy on her first Christmas with a tree that she would remember. I put photos of her on Facebook.

She loved it when I showed her all the likes, love symbols, and kind words that people said about her, from her church on Facebook family.

These were people she had not seen in months since she fell. She had over thirty years in her church ministry. She worked in many positions such as teaching, and became a Deacon, and member of the prayer team for over fifteen years.

Johnnie and her disability

She had a brain tumor that left her with her left side paralyzed. She found someone who accepted her and will always be a friend and a savior. She loves so many verses and is very loyal to her Pastors and her church.

Johnnie felt, in February of 2023, that the good years of the church had ended. She had not been able to live alone so she lived with me.,

Adjustments were made time for her to live with me again

She does not remember being back in her old room here at the house. She said sometimes it comes and goes, she has a small vision of the house she moved back into. She enjoys watching TV and eating.

She is used to being alone at her apartment, so she stays in her room most of the time. She feels lost with her memory lost to dementia.

It is hard to watch her go through this again.

She has been through so much with the loss of her left side, but she has been one of the most independent women of God I have ever known.

My sister Johnnie was a faithful wife, sister, mother, and friend.

I would love to continue, there is so much to say about the end life of a person who loves God so much. And he had blessed her with her independence for a long time.

She worshiped under the minister of Pastors, her brother for over thirty years. She was a faithful woman of God.

It had been five months since she left the church and she forgot a lot but one thing she said was she did not want to lose her memory of God!

I pray it never happens. She is my twin. I have always been her big sister, even if she is the oldest and I will care for her until I am too old continue.

I pray her final days will be here at home.

But as time passes, I wonder if she will make it to Christmas to enjoy a beautiful Christmas at my home.

Johnnie's brain is losing memory fast and she is not able to re-member what is happening from moment to moment. It breaks my heart; I will try to get her to church but will someone bring her home. This is a challenging task for me. She loves church and rarely misses a Sunday.

She went to church a couple of times to visit her sister's friend from church. Even stayed over for a cookout with her prayer team.

I felt it might be the last time for over thirty years. My daughter drove us back through our life in the past, more specifically, 1965.

She sings the music of some of her favorite Vocal Group "The Temptation" alone and cries over these moments. The song "My Girl", we drove to Zion Beach she did not remember. We drove on Market St in Waukegan, a place they used to hang out after hours across the railroad track. It was all demolished. We drove to two locations where she used to eat, all demolished, and no longer there.

Since 1965, a lot of places and people have moved or are dead. The South Side of Waukegan was gone due to this and other rea-sons. Not much left of the past, the house we lived in was gone.

South Avenue was the location where our house used to be.

Now it's a children's playground. The grocery store is gone.

The place where she got married to her first husband, who was from an upper-class family. Before she became disabled life was picture-perfect but after the stroke, it changed.

Dementia has taken away her independent life, she is one of the most powerful strong-willed women I have ever known.

Johnnie, my sister and best friend, was slowly leaving in front of my eyes. It was painful to see her go.

It is painful to watch someone you love lose all the memories of their life and those she loved. I had endured so much pain with the loss of my oldest grandson at 23 years old.

His mother, my daughter, is going in and out of hospitals, suffering.

But I would see it through until the end, somehow, my life changed and I now had to look after Johnnie as if she was a child who could not be left alone.

But she still managed to get dressed and make her bed. She controlled herself with one hand. Even though her whole left side was of no use to her, she would drag it around with pride.

My Sister Johnnie was so special to me. I could not understand how this could happen to such a kind-hearted person like Johnnie. She is named after her father Johnny. Her name was spelled differently because of her gender but if she were a boy, she would be a split end image of her father.

However, she had her mother's smile, we both had her smile.

August 2, 2023, around 9:30 a.m., she was in the kitchen at my home, now her home.

She fell and broke her arm. I was sitting in the kitchen and my daughter was standing near her. She was getting her coffee to take to her room. She had done this most of her adult life.

But this would be her final stay here. I had made other choices to keep her safe like closing my office and staying home with her at my age. I knew I could not do it any longer, she would forget me.

She would soon be gone, I had to find the best care I could for her.

I had to face the fact that I was too old to deal with her alone. My health was not so good, I started working as a Caregiver, making 156 dollars a week, four hours a day, which was just supposed to have been temporary, but things changed, I started in September, and I still am her Caregiver with the same hours. Even if I worked 24 hours, I only got 12 hours a week pay so she had to help with the bills so I could afford to leave my coaching business to care for her losing income. But because of our bond and closeness, we stay together. My husband could not drive because he lost part of his eyesight in 2004. I was tired of doing all the driving, I am getting old as well. But somehow until the day comes for her to be removed from home, my home will always be her home. We had to face the fear of the unknown together.

- During the time I had my coaching business a kind older lady around my age came to my office and asked if could I find a caregiver for her mom.

- I had worked in the field for a long time and I was told her mother was special. She wanted someone like me to care for her. I had another client but I promised her I would meet her Mom.

- She was the wife of a retired Pastor who had relocated to another church to do some work in ministry. They need me for just one day to sit and watch her. I met Freda at her daughter's beautiful home and l loved her from day one when she was 96 years old. She was a pleasant person to be around. She obeys her daughter's rules most of the time. It was an easy September, a nice calm day, she was white, and I was black. She is from the South. We lived different lives, she was raised on a farm with her family, mother, and father, on the other hand, I lived with my mother out in the Country with fields and trees.

- Despite this, we found so much in common. She did not know that much about black people and I did not know much about white people. We knew there were good and evil in both.

- We both grew up going to church, her mother stayed home on Sunday and my mother went to church every Sunday after relocating north, every day in there, and took us with her. Her dad took them to church, with her, and her siblings. We talked every Sunday about church, food, and so much more of my life.

But the good part about it was that it was a happy time in life for both of us. One day, she had short-term memory but she would talk a lot about her mom and dad's past life growing up in Tennessee. And once after her cat died, we had that conversation no more. She stopped talking and soon passed away. Her cat was family. She was with her for fourteen years.

I miss her. She was blessed to have a daughter to bring her and take care of her. She did a beautiful job and she is in a beautiful place.

With this painful disease slowly eating their brain away, they live but are mostly brain-dead. It's hell to watch daily as this happens to your loved one. Living with Dementia is hell on earth for all of us who have to live with it and those who take care of loved ones with Dementia. She, helped me to to deal with my own sister

God knew and he sent me to her .for the experience and knowledge, with her loving family I learn a lot I will always be thankful.

Hell On Earth Living With Dementia.

The most fatal form of dementia Is Creutzfeldt-Jakob disease (CDJ) a rare and fatal form of dementia, caused by abnormal prison proteins that are toxic to the brain? Creutzfeldt-Jakob disease, a type of dementia that gets worse unusually fast, is a more common cause of dementia, such as Alzheimer's dementia with levy bodies and frontotemporal dementia, typically progressing more slowly.

Through a process scientists do not yet understand, misfolded prion protein destroys. brain cells, resulting in damage that leads to a rapid decline in thinking and reasoning as well as involuntary muscle movements. Confusion, difficulty walking, and mood changes.

Experts recognize the following main types of Creutzfeldt-Jakob disease. The first appears between ages 60 and 65. Medical procedures involving instruments used in neurosurgery, growth hormones from human sources, or certain transplanted human tissues. To find out more about this disease look it up on goggles.

Some of the most common Depression Agitation, apathy, and mood swings Rapidly worsening confusion.

Problems with memory, thinking, planning, and thinking.

Difficulty walking Muscle stiffness twitches and involatile jerky movement Vision problems such as double vision hallucinations.

To live with this kind of suffering must be hell on earth for some of us.

Dementia is a progressive disease, so it will gradually get worse over time. However, external factors, such as a brain injury or sudden change in routine, can trigger sudden worsening of dementia symptoms.

When should someone be hospitalized?

For example, a hospital admission, a career becoming ill, and being unable to care for the person safety concerns about the person with dementia experiencing behaviors that challenge, such as being awake all night or becoming aggressive, or agitated.

Dementia is a broad term for a decline in mental abilities that lasts a long time or does not end symptoms include memory loss, trouble making decisions, and changes in behavior, 60% -80% of dementia cases have Alzheimer's Over 5 million Americans have Alzheimer's.

The 6th most significant cause of mortality in the US.

Alzheimer's and other progressive dementias are incurable even though the disease gets worse over time and how long it takes can vary significantly from one patient to the next.

Changing personalities and dem can make caring for a loved one difficult and uncomfortable.

They might even forget who their closest friends and family are. Dementia requires excellent care and being a family caregiver, you must detect dementia patient dying signs Hospice in this regard provides physical, emotional, and spiritual care to patients and families where they live.

This article talks about the seven stages of dementia so that you know what to expect if you or a loved one has been diagnosed.

The stages are as follows:

1. No cognitive decline
2. Very mid-cognitive decline

3. Mild cognitive decline

4. Moderate cognitive decline

5. Moderately severe cognitive decline

6. Severe cognitive decline

7. Very severe cognitive decline

This website was extremely helpful melodiacare.com

I share what I know according to what the medical study tells us about these signs.

Let us read them.

The 7 Stages of Decline

1. No cognitive decline, the person has no memory loss, confusion, or cognitive impairment at this stage. However, as brain neurons die and lose connections, their structure and function decline.

Stage 2: very mid Cognitive Decline

The person starts to have occasional memory gaps, such as:

Misplacing everyday items Forgetting familiar names Symptoms are unlikely to influence job or social interactions at this stage.

For instance, if the patient can pass a memory test during a clinical interview, the symptoms may be too minor to identify.

Stage 3: Mild cognitive Decline

At this stage, cognitive impairment becomes apparel to the patient, friends' family, and colleagues.

Symptoms include:

1. Walking or driving lost, especially in unfamiliar places.
2. Reading and forgetting.
3. Having trouble remembering the names of people they have just met.
4. Losing things of importance or value
5. Problem-focusing and completing complex tasks
6. Increasing social difficulties
7. Increasing social diffiulties
8. Forgetting words and family names often
9. Poor work performance that colleagues notice

As a person's symptoms become more apparent and get in the way of their ability to work, they may feel anxious.

Stage 4: Moderate cognitive Decline

In this stage, a clinical interview will show a noticeable decline in the person's mental abilities.

This stage may cause:

Unawareness of recent events.

Trouble recalling personal history.

Problems planning, traveling, and managing expenses.

At this point, the person will be able to remember the names and faces of loved ones and get around familiar places. They may avoid stressful events to avoid anxiety and hide their distress.

Stage 5: Moderately Severe Cognitive Decline

From this stage on, the person may no longer be able to do things independently.

Symptoms include:

Trouble remembering their address phone number, or high school.

Confusion over the season, date of the week, or time.

Difficulty counting backward from 20 by 2s or 40s by 4s (if educated and one table):

Decision-making issues.

The person may remember their name, their spouses, and their children's but not their grandchildren's. They may need help dressing but not eating or using the bathroom.

Stage 6: Severe Cognitive Decline

At this point, the person may need a lot of care because they are showing signs of like:

Trouble remembering their spouse, children, or primary care and lack of awareness of all.

Of the recent events and situations in their life Trouble counting to 10 either backward or forwards. Unawareness of time location, and surrounds Unable to travel without assistance Wandering tendencies.

The person may go through changes in their feelings and personalities, such as:

Paranoia, hallucinations, and delusions, such as talking to themselves or thinking that their caregivers want to hurt them.

Obsessive signs, such as cleaning something over and over Anxiety, irritability, and even dangerous behavior Loss of willpower because you cannot hold on to a thought long enough to finish the action.

The person may remember their name and discriminate between familiar and unfamiliar people during this period. They may need help with tasks of daily living, and they may have problems with incontinence and sleeping.

Stage 7: Very Severe Cognitive Decline

In the last stage, the brain loses contact with the body and can no longer tell it what to do.

The person may lose the ability to move and talk over time. They might only be able to make sounds or say things that cannot be understood. Eating, walking, and using the bathroom will require help.

Tip for Managing Dementia's Final Signs

Caregivers must watch for signs of pain or discomfort in severe dementia patients, who typically have trouble communicating.

Moreover, moaning screaming, restlessness grimacing, and sweating are some of the signs. Hospice or palliative care may also be needed to treat pain.

Hospice can provide a hospital bed or equipment to help end-stage dementia patients sit up.

Families struggle most when a dementia patient can no longer eat or drink Dementia patients commonly try to remove feeding tubes or IV drips, causing discomfort and infection instead, make sure the person is relaxed They can make their final transition in tranquility if they receive mouth care to prevent they are from drying out.

Helping your loved one as a person gets worse, you can help them by being there for them in a loving and caring way. Set them for them. hold hands and play their music.

Helping a loved one organize their company's affairs is one of the best things.

You can do for them Establish financial and healthcare powers of attorney to make decisions when your loved one cannot function. Look into funeral plans before you need them, so you do not have to make important choices in a crisis.

Talk to your loved one's doctor about home palliative care and hospice care when they are ready.

How can Hospice Help with the latest Stages of Dementia?

Hospice care will ease caregiving's physical and mental stress and help you spot dementia-related signs that indicate death.

Nurses can update medicines and care treatments as needed. Aides can help with bathing, cleaning, and other personal tasks. Social workers organize patient and family resources. Chaplains and bereavement specialists can assist with emotional and spiritual needs. Family members might also contact hospice without waiting for the doctor's recommendation. melodica Care Hospice can benefit dementia patients and their families by providing information about hospice eligibility and scheduling consultations. I did this because it is extremely hard to witness someone close to you losing their mind. This information was listed on the Google website.

Some can agree with the circle of atonement that traditions have a name for the place where people are punished for the crimes or sins they committed it is a place they go after they die, where they are attacked with various forms of suffering, an abode where they are separated from goodness and love, a state which the book of Revelation in the Bible calls the second death what is the name of this place? It is, of course, hell and since our world matches this description so well, it is difficult not to conclude that this place is hell. Objections to realizing that this place is hell. Now there is more data out here you can find on Google and other websites. These are some of the major points that Impeded, to understand that because of parents' choices, the sin really, does fall on the parent. The suffering, we endure for letting emotion become love and love become sexual pleasure. Humans sometimes feed off sex and love.

This is just some data on the life left behind that will never get out of this eternal hell lock inside the mind.

The mercy of God is fading slowly, and we will be lost even more we will not survive this end before we had so much to build on but today most Americans, dream is fading, and our faith in God too.

We have lost the passion for what is right!

Some of us go through every day with pain, taking lots of medication but never getting any better, pain on a daily affects the brain, and your moods, but to top it off you become dependent on the drugs. This torture and hell on earth Living in fear of being beaten for love.

Sickness, and mental illness, on a daily, is hell, and everything else comes with it. Living in poverty is hell on earth. Being rejected and living alone for the rest of your life is hell on earth.

My return to Zion on 31ST.

In 1998, all I had to do was move to a brand-new home, no one had bought the land the old homes that used to be there were gone except a few homes it looked so different there were no rock roads.

They built an apartment building next to it.

I did not want to be here, but the profit was for me to return just like the voice in my head would say you will not die you will return to 31 Street when we closed on the house, I saw a no Trusting passing sign in the yard.

I was sick at that time, and taking a lot of medications. I would leave for work at that time. I was driving a big school bus, sometimes I would drive 20 minutes to park my bus.

I would come around the back and it was like the garden of evil so green and beautiful I felt at home this house was for sale my husband knew the person that had the house she showed it to us but we had no money to buy a house but we did it was already set for me to move in the realtor said when went told her the story of my father coming her in a dream while I was in the house we were able to close quickly and move in I felt blessed, not know there were storms coming and I would have to pay the price for this knowledge of life this pain, this was my inner strength to keep me grounded. I was a dreamer. I wanted to be rich cause I thought being poor made you unhappy not having enough, you learn to be thankful for having food and a place to live.

I was sixteen when I decided to run away with the man of my dreams not knowing I was living with the devil he made my life a living hell for about ten years with all kinds of abuse from the night I jumped in his car and headed back to Mississippi I loved him and wanted to believe him when said he loved me.

But like the spirit of God spoke to me in my head and said that I would travel, see a lot, and experience a lot and I would return to 31st In the city of Zion IL

What a place to start the fall of 1965 when we moved to Zion I believe. We lived in a two-bedroom house with 10 children, I was ready to get out.

After my mom and dad accused me of sleeping in the car with

my boyfriend. I went mad and wanted to run, he wanted, to get away from God, and the church, our family was big on church. with and marriage. This, the demon of drinking, and fighting, entered us like a passion, we had to have, and it did Destroy his mind. He later turns to drugs. And died. I often wonder if we were chosen and we paid the price, for ten years together.

There was something about 31st I did not come back to see, my mother, the land was taken for city taxes. I did not want to be here,

A new rebuilt house,wow this was on the land I ran away from. A promise God spoke to me.

So much happened so many years ago, I cannot write it all in one book. My life is a library with so many stories, and things I have done and seen. As I was promised.

But I disobeyed My parent and I had to pay the price. I ran away.

I left never to return to my Parent's home. I was grown up; I moved back here in 1992 after leaving for two to Alabama.

I never thought about Zion, my parents no longer lived in Zion why would I come back?

I got pregnant with my oldest of two daughters, it was my first. I was 29 a new mother, and the lifestyle I lived was for family, everybody in Hollywood was living in the fast lane. So, I drove back home I still did not think about the voice coming back to Zion, for what? I lived with my sister, Johnnie, until my daughter was born.

THE GIRL THAT DREAME
MOST OF HER LIFE

She dreamed of a different life in another time and place:

Let's face it, if you were born in 1951 things would be different, things are not the same today as they were in the fifties and sixties American dreams were different for African American families living in the United States of America.

Most African Americans believed in God, and had dreams that one day, their God would save them!

She dreamed of love as being beautiful on the other side of hate, born into this world an African American child in a world of racist white people.

Her parents could not read, they may have had dreams of many things.

The dream that could be true for her mom, was when her father came back and rescued them. It was too late the damage had been done.

She was abused by her stepfather her mother believed him, not her.

At night she would have horrified dreams it was always dark, and something, or someone, was always chasing her.

She dreams, the same dream at some point she would meet up with this same big black bear, chasing her. It was revealed years later that a demon was present, in the form of a bear. her childhood fear was manifested in her mind after reading about big angry bears in storybooks, and old folks' tales.

She was running from the truth she was running for her life waking up feeling like she had never slept.

In her daytime dreams, she sometimes made up stories to make her happy.

There were times when she would share her thoughts just to make her younger brother, and sisters happy, if only for a minute.

She would search for thoughts, in her mind that would make them laugh, when they had every reason to cry.

She would say things like, we are a rich family they would role-play reverse with the character of the boss man, the plantation owner, and his family. they would laugh, and mock them, the way they mocked and treated the African families.

She dreamed; they ate what they wanted to eat, whenever they wanted to eat, but this was only in her daydreams.

She dreamed of one day being free of poverty, and being able to vote, in the election of the United States of America. One day her dream came true, and she now has a choice.

She dreamed of not being black, but instead a beautiful woman, with wisdom and knowledge, and yes" that was a dream in the fifties and sixties.

Everything else belonged to her in her head: and no one could take her dreams from her.

THE GIRL THAT DREAMED
MOST OF HER LIFE!

She woke up!

She woke up to the truth!

There are no other places, to go to find the things she dreamed of because she lived in the United States? she was born in the United States, where all the things she believed to be in her head, were not true. Now she would never escape her nightmares. Because she lived in a country as big, and ugly as the bear.

Manifesting a new kind of fear, the kind of fear, that was mixed and confused about race, greed, and more.

She woke up to the fact, that America was the home of the descendants' children, of her forefathers who were still slaves in their minds, ln hell on earth.

Her race of people was called by many names, such as a Negro, Nigger, Colored, Black, Slaves, and last, African Americans.

She woke up to the truth about love, hate, abuse, racism, Justice, democracy, politics, marriage, divorce, poverty, and sickness.

She woke up and now she could deal with the rejection, and fears, that she lived with and ran from.

She was very aware of the curse on her life but how would she get rid of the curse how?

For she believed in nothing, she trusted no one.

She lived a very isolated life. Her fears, of her curse, are activated in her daughters' lives, and the lives, of their children.

People believe that curses, are of the devil and he possesses the power of negative energy, space, and time on this planet,

And that God, had recused them like he had rescued her forefathers, at death.

Death was the only way they were free. They were born under the curse.

The curse stayed with them until death, at death, they left poverty, love, family, children, friends, suffering, and everything in this world they were free at last!

She woke up to a feeling of fear that would lead her to choose the wrong mate, the wrong life, and the wrong path she chose to stay in a life of suffering because she was under the curse.

That was the only choice she had, until she believed, that she could break the curse, but how?

She found out her ancestors believed in God, and that he would lead them to the promised land.

For some of them, the promised land meant when we lived here.

She believed that the reason why African Americans, suffer is because they feel unworthy of God's love.

She believed that they believed it was God's will that they suffer. Our ancestors, had to suffer, at the hands of God's chosen one the white man. he beat it in them, to free them of suffering, he told them that God would take their souls, with Him!

African American churches and the population grew, and their dreams, and hopes, were in the hands of God!

They prayed and the churches grew.

More women, pastors, Praise teams, dancers, they all grew.

Black organizations were moving forward as well.

In 2020 the churches shut down, and many African American families did not return to church.

They were more confused than ever.

Fear gripped the nation, and the lack of faith in God was unbelievable. I knew they had failed the curse, and were recreated a new curse, an unforgivable curse until death.

She believes that they would not find freedom or a beautiful place at death.

She knew that the dreams she once had were all in her head and she could dream of peace, love, and wealth, whenever she wanted to.

She believed that the curse that she was born with was broken. Even if we fail the overall test of faith in God, during the Covid season.

Those that were left here have a chance to keep or break, the curse.

This would be the only way they, will know the beauty of peace, and love A peaceful life, on this planet earth., and a peaceful life, on this planet earth.

They would have to know, that dreams come with no price attached to their faith, and having unlimited beliefs would bring the American dream, alive once again, and forevermore, the African American race, has paid the price they believe it to be paid in full. They would have to know, that dreams come with no price attached to their faith, and having unlimited beliefs, would bring the American dream alive once again, and forevermore.

PART THREE: THE GIRL WHO DREAMED MOST OF HER LIFE

She dreams of owning her own women's fashion store, the first one she had ever seen was a store that burst her heart, with delight.

Young & hard in the world of fashion, it is like walking out of a dream and living the dream in the daytime.

This was real, she thought it was an awesome job, and she would take it but as beautiful, and exciting as it was, she knew she would pay a price that was not attached to the contract, the price was abuse, and sexual harassment from the owner.

She had the choice, to stay or leave but because she was used to dreaming and waking up. She would wake up and go back to day-dreaming.

She loved the feeling of power, she had to erase the evil thoughts of guilt and shame, and it worked for her because she was used to being rejected.

Very little works out for her. She will create the next dream, and she will leave this one behind. To refresh it when needed.

She Could control her feelings, and emotions of dealing with fear, sadness, pain, regrets, rejection, and the list goes on.

Just being here was a full-time job.

Ideas, about opening her own women's shop, popped up in her head, at night erasing the fear of the bear, that came every night.

She was sure she had left that bear behind a long time ago and moved on.

She woke up! To

Forty years and more of pain, and suffering. She would dream no more.

Life was real, she lived in hell on earth!

She will not die here, she will rise and save lives, as a life coach,

Her, reason for becoming a life coach is Her life and the lives of others, her life was worth the fight and the daily battles for A very long time.

Every life is the same to God! Life is worth saving so you can be all God indented, you too be.

You will wake up because!

I saw so much suffering, in this world it had to be hell or like hell.

My name is Ruthie Caples Spates, I am the Girl who dreamed, most of her life!

www.ingramcontent.com/pod-product-compliance
Lightning Source LLC
Chambersburg PA
CBHW051550120626
46551CB00013B/1457